This book belongs to:

_____

How to Solve a Problem Like

Physical Verbal Emotional

BULLYING

Neeti Kohli, M.D.

To order additional copies of this book, contact:

Awareness Books for Children
P.O. Box 2495
Edmond, Oklahoma 73083-2495

Phone: 1-405-330-8888
Fax: 1-405-330-8880

Website: www.awarenessbooksforchildren.org

My special thanks to:

My husband Vivek and
my children Uday & Supriya

Randy Anderson

Ralonda Wood

Kristi Kenney

Wayne Stein

Family & Friends

A note to all the adults

Bullying is a big issue today. One child becomes a bully and the other child becomes a victim. Both situations are not good.

It is important to teach a child how to handle a bully. At the same time, it is important to prevent more bullies from being formed. This book helps a child in both ways. It focuses on equality, boosting a child's confidence, empathy, judgment, and differentiating between right and wrong.

No matter how confident a child is, it is very difficult for a child to change the behavior of a bully. A child needs support from adults. Adults are powerful. If a child doesn't get the help that he or she needs, then a child may become depressed or may also become a bully.

Adults should be able to judge and take action to support the honest and good side of children. Support from an adult is extremely important in bringing about a change.

Let us get together to support what is righteous, kind, and ethical.

Neeti Kohli, M.D.

We all are special.

We all are precious.

We all have a wonderful heart.

We all want to be loved by others.

All children want to be loved by others, have friends to play with, and be treated nicely. Within all of us is the same good heart that wants to love and help others. Aren't we all the same?

A Good Heart

Each one of us is precious!

Every good heart has a different body. Our bodies are like costumes which are made of different looks and talents. Every good heart wears a different looking costume.

Our body
or
a costume

Every good heart gets a different costume to wear.

No one is allowed to choose a costume. It is a gift that is given to us.

We all look different from outside, but from inside…

We all have the same desire to be loved, respected, and accepted. Therefore, we are all alike and equal.

 = 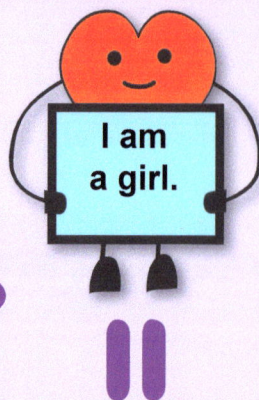 = 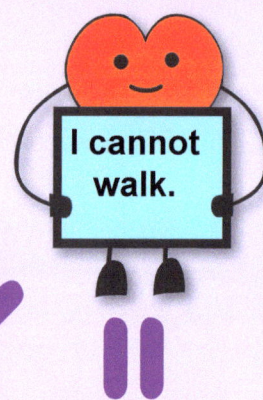 =

 =  = 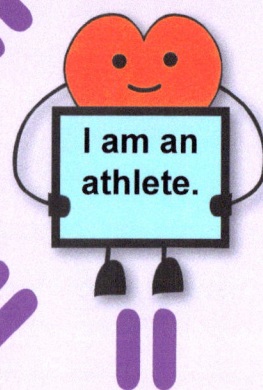 =

 =  = 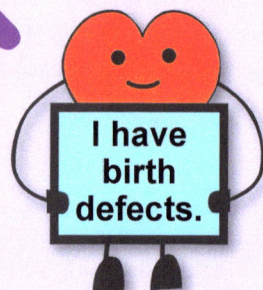 =

No matter how our peers look from outside, we should see the same good and loving heart within all children.

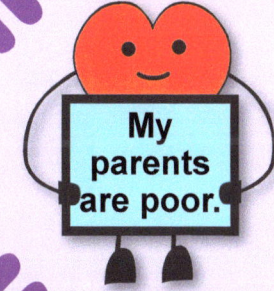

Because we all are alike inside, we deserve to be treated with equality, love, and respect.

We have the right to play together!

Some of us may still become bullies.

Alert!
Anyone can
become a bully!

Bullies repeatedly:

- Are mean to others.

- Hurt others physically or emotionally on purpose.

- Pretend to be stronger and better than others.

- Put others down.

This is how it all begins…

Every bully is also born with a good heart.
He or she is one of us.

Rad received a car for his birthday. He loved to share it with his friends.

Something can happen in our life that can change our behavior.
Someone may hurt us, leave us alone, or make us sad.
Perhaps no one was there to listen to our problems.

York came and pulled the toy away from Rad's hand. Rad became sad. No one was there to listen about his pain.

We do not want to be hurt. So we try to defend ourselves. It is good to protect ourselves and say what is right. However, in the process of protecting ourselves, sometimes we overdo it, and become mean and hurt others.

Rad wanted his toy back. In anger, he pushed York very hard to get it back. He felt strong, in control, and powerful.

It is all right to have an argument or even a small fight once in a while. But when we begin to hurt others again and again, then it becomes bad. The badness doesn't know where to stop. It becomes worse and worse, the good heart hides, and a bully is born.

Then, Rad started to hurt other children too. He started to snatch their toys, hit them, and call them names. From a good boy, Rad became a bully "monster."

Also, we seek attention when we are jealous of someone, doubt our own potential, or lack confidence. Hurting others can sometimes make us feel strong, powerful, and popular. Therefore, we may continue to bully. But we all know that this is not right.

One simple question to ask ourself can help us a lot.

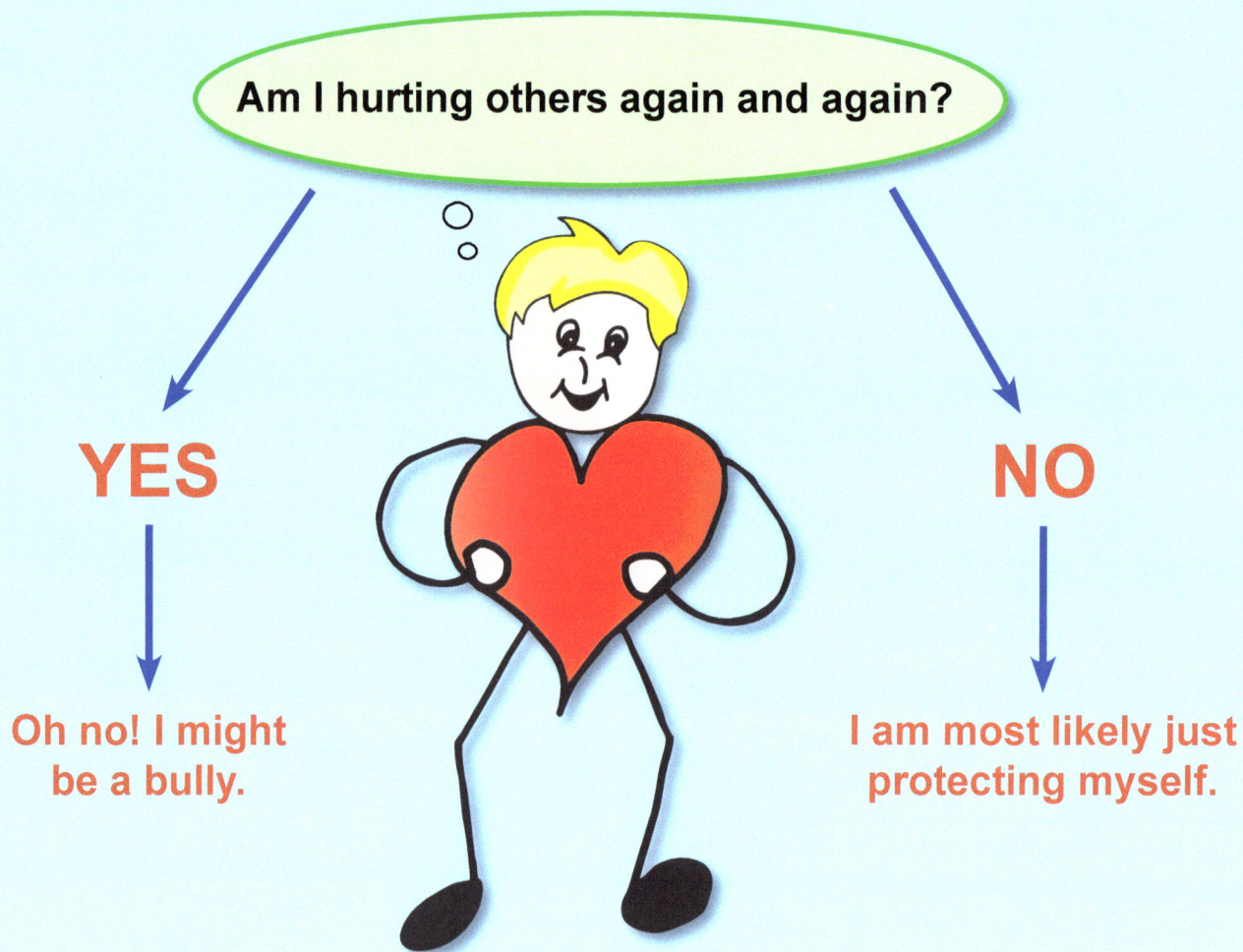

Am I hurting others again and again?

YES

NO

Oh no! I might be a bully.

I am most likely just protecting myself.

Protecting ourselves is good, but repeatedly hurting others is bullying.

What Can a Bully Do?

A bully can:

- **Physically** hurt us by hitting, kicking, pushing, or throwing things at us.

- **Verbally** make fun of us by making bad comments on how we look or what we wear.

- **Emotionally** hurt us by speaking badly about us, criticizing us, spreading rumors about us, or stopping others from being friends with us.

What can a Cyberbully do?

A Cyberbully can:

Use the Internet to bully us by writing hateful and threatening messages or emails, spreading rumors about us on the Internet, posting wrong images, stealing our identity, and writing messages in our name.

Rumors and images can spread fast, and they can stay on the Internet forever. This can severely hurt our feelings and make us sad.

How can we solve this problem of bullying?

WE CAN MAKE A DIFFERENCE!

We should always remember that we all have different capabilities. Each one of us is unique. No one is superior or inferior to the other. If someone tells us that we are bad or awful, we know that it is not true. We should not let negative statements about us make us sad.

We should always assess the situation and then act accordingly.
We can choose to do what is best for us.

One simple question to ask ourself.

Can I speak in front of the bully?

YES
I am confident.

NO
Bully is too strong.
I cannot say anything.

STOP IT!

**Tell a bully to stop.
Inform an adult.**

**Ignore and walk away.
Inform an adult.**

Ignoring and walking away does not make us weak.
We are still confident, proud, and strong.

We should <u>always inform</u> an adult even if a bully says not to inform anyone. A bully can become stronger if we hide and not tell anyone. If we tell an adult, then we will feel appreciated. Also, an adult can keep it a secret. The bully may never come to know that we have shared the information.

Adults (Parents, Teachers, Counselors, Principals) can do a lot of things to help us.

Adults Can:

- Tell bullies what they are doing wrong.

- Talk to the bullies' parents to make them correct their behavior.

- Punish bullies if they do not listen and correct their behavior.

- Send bullies to a counselor, psychologist, or doctor to modify their behavior.

Our parents are caring and powerful. They can inform our teachers, counselors, or principals. They can even approach the U.S. Department of Education.

A bully may be strong in front of us…

…but a bully is weak in front of an adult.

We should <u>always be kind and help others</u>.

When we are being bullied, all we want is the help and support from someone who is close by.

When we see someone being bullied, all we need to do is to help and support that person.

Never leave a bullied child alone!

We can help a child who is being bullied by:

- Telling a child who is bullying to "STOP."

- Informing an adult.

- Talking to a child who is crying.

- Playing with the child who was bullied.

Love Respect Support Help Each Other

Our love and togetherness can create a good environment in which everyone is respectful and helpful to each other. Such an environment can also help a bully to become a good child again.

SUCCESS

GREAT

BRIGHT FUTURE

We are friends now!

Bully Rad

Someone told Rad to "STOP."

Better Rad

Rad received love and affection from friends.

Good Rad

We love each other.
We care for each other.
We share with each other.
We help each other.

We are good children.
We are happy children.
Come join us!

AWARENESS CLUB
FOR CHILDREN

www.ingramcontent.com/pod-product-compliance
Lightning Source LLC
LaVergne TN
LVHW072105070426
835508LV00003B/276